TEACHING GUIDE
for

SONGS FOR LITTLE ONES

Translations, Activities, and Drawings by:

Silvia León

Cover Illustration by:

Krystina Ponce de León (age 6)

Collection 1 Written & Prepared By:
Silvia León / Smarty Kat Designs
Produced By:
Shawn Brooke Enterprises
22916 Styles Street
Woodland Hills, CA 91367

Verses to certain songs and rhymes in this booklet may or may not be in the corresponding cassette, Songs for Little Ones/Canciones Para Pequeños.

For Krystopher, my son, Michael, my nephew, and Krystina, my niece . . . my constant reminders of the importance in preserving the magical experiences of childhood that are necessary for the survival of the human spirit in every adult.

I S B N 0-9643490-0-0

Copyright © 1995 Smarty Kat Designs

All rights reserved

Shaun Brooke Enterprises
22916 Styles Street
Woodland Hills, CA 91367

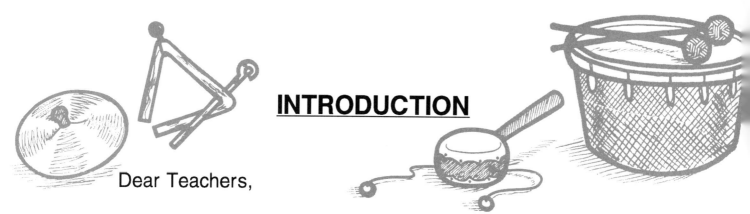

INTRODUCTION

Dear Teachers,

I am a bilingual preschool teacher for the School Readiness Language Development Program (SRLDP) for the Los Angeles Unified School District. Many years ago I began translating nursery songs, rhymes, and fingerplays out of complete frustration since there were no available early childhood materials in Spanish. In the beginning, I encountered many obstacles: I didn't know anything about musical notes (I still don't!) I couldn't play any musical instruments, and Lord knows, I was no poet. Furthermore, I feared my students, teacher assistant, and parent volunteers would laugh at my singing and autoharp attempts. I needed courage -- and lots of it.

As a very young child, I remembered the happy feelings that I felt inside when I lay together with my grandfather on a hammock singing old Spanish love songs before the afternoon siesta. I also remembered the joy of listening and dancing to the rhythmic patterns of the conga drums, maracas, claves, and guiro that rumbled throughout my mother's house as I was growing up. The memories of those happy musical moments that I had experienced as a child ignited the fire I needed to build my courage and pass on these happy feelings to my preschoolers.

To build up my musical self-confidence, I bought wonderful books, records, and tapes. I can't remember when or how, but one day I reached for that old dusty autoharp and began playing and singing a one chord song. It didn't matter that I sang off key, nor that my autoharp was somewhat out of tune.

My four-year old students thought that I was great . . . and nobody laughed! I have tuned my autoharp and polished my singing since then; however, the moral of the story is . . . you can never improve on something you have never begun!

This booklet contains songs and rhymes that have survived the test of time with the little ones. They have been translated from English to Spanish, and from Spanish to English so that the children who speak either of these languages can equally enjoy them. You will find lesson plans, related literature, and extended activities that will connect the songs and rhymes with other areas of the early childhood curriculum. There are twelve flannel board felt sets, one for each song or rhyme, plus the cassette, "Songs for Little ones / Canciones Para Pequeños", that have been specifically designed to accompany this booklet. However, if you are familiar with these popular songs and rhymes, all you will need to do is to make your own flannel board or puppet visuals.

I hope this booklet is useful and FUN in your classrooms. If you have any questions, please write or call me at

ShawnBrooke Enterprises
Producer of SMARTY KAT Felt Materials
22916 Styles Street
Woodland Hills, CA 91367
(800) 995-1353

Best wishes always!!

Silvia León

TABLE OF CONTENTS

APPLICATIONS ACROSS THE CURRICULUM

The Traditional Finger rhymes and songs presented in <u>all</u> of these sets provide an excellent way to develop language in the young child. Language development is accomplished through the repetitious nature of the rhymes and songs and through memorization. This method works exceptionally well in both bilingual and ESL settings.

We have found that by presenting the units suggested below using these rhymes, songs and their felt characters as the catalyst, the child can become actively involved in the entire early education curriculum.

Below are some specific concepts that are covered in each unit and the Smarty Kat sets that are applicable. Included in all the units are opportunities to enhance language development, related literature, music, movement, rhythms, cooking, and art. Be sure to check the lesson guide for each unit for more detailed information.

Weather Unit - Use **Mr. Sun**

    Types of weather - sunny, cloudy, windy, rainy
    Rain cycle
    Weather sounds
    Colors of sun, snow, rainbow
    Appropriate dress

Units of the Body, Myself - Use **Head & Shoulders, Thumbkin and 10 Children**
    Names of body parts, where they are and how they move
    Following directions - positioning body parts in the correct location
    Colors of : eyes, hair, skin, etc.
    Shapes of : eyes, nose, or face
    Sizes: large, medium, small (height, size of hands and feet)
    Likes and differences
    Finger names
    Hand functions
    Sense of touch
    Naming: child's own name, names of family members, and classmates
    Math skills: recognition of numerals: 0 - 10, counting (of children or body parts)
       and counting in American Sign Language
    Teaching positions and the ability to follow directions: next to, in front of, in back of,
       below, above, etc.*
    Recognizing ordinal numbers: 1st, 2nd, 3rd.....last*
    Compare and contrast: individual differences
    Reinforce social skills: acceptance of and helping others and working together

Fruits and Vegetable and Fall Unit - Use **5 Little Pumpkins**

    Math skills: counting, ordinal numbers, estimation, and graphing
    Colors, shapes, sizes
    Categorizing
    Expression of emotions and feelings
    Where and how they grow and taste
    Lead into the Farm Unit

Farm Unit - Use **5 Little Pumpkins, Baby Chicks, 6 Little Ducks, 5 Speckled Frogs and Eency Weency Spider**

Study egg laying animals
Colors
Identify and naming: animals and family members
Sounds animals make
Math skills: counting skills, ordinal numbers, numeral recognition, subtraction
Sizes
Likes and differences: of chicks and ducks
Living habitats
Frog study
Insect study
Pond habitat
Spider study
Voice pitch changes

Frogs and Spiders can live on the farm or in the rain forest. These two sets can be used as your transition from the farm to the rain forest unit.

Rain Forest Unit - Use **5 Little Monkeys Jumping on a Bed and 5 Little Monkeys Sitting in a Tree**

Math skills: numeral recognition, counting, subtractions, addition, concepts of sets
Colors
Learning positions: in, under, on, above, next to etc.*
Following directions
Comparison concepts (numbers in tails and number of bananas)
Monkey study
Crocodile study
Fact vs. fantasy*

Space Unit - Use **Twinkle Star**

Study of stars and planets
Simple space study
Understanding daytime and nighttime
Shapes: of stars, moon, planets, and diamond

The use of these sets in conjunction with the early education curriculum is limited <u>ONLY</u> by the individual imagination and creativity.

* See Additional Activities for more detailed instructions on pages 81 & 82.

V

CONTENTS BY SUBJECT

FIVE LITTLE MONKEYS JUMPING ON THE BED

Traditional

Five little monkeys jumping on the bed.

One fell off and bumped his head.

The mama called the doctor

And the doctor said,

"No more monkeys jumping on the bed!"

Four little monkeys...

Three little monkeys...

Two little monkeys...

One little monkey...

Zero monkeys jumping on the bed.

None fell off and bumped their heads.

The mama called the doctor

And the doctor said,

"Put those monkeys back into bed!"

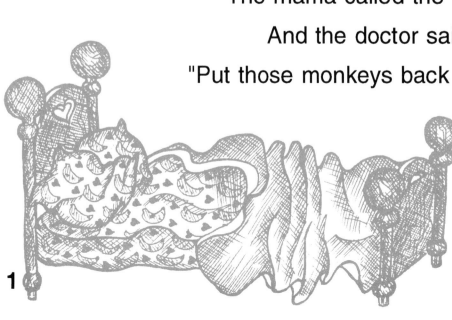

1

CINCO MONITOS BRINCANDO EN LA CAMA

Translation by Silvia León

Cinco *monitos
Brincando en la cama,
Brincando en la cama,
La cama de la **mama.
Uno se cayó y la cabeza se golpió.
Mamá llamó al doctor y él dijo,
"¡Que Horror! No más monos brincando,
Por favor!"

Cuatro monitos...
Tres monitos...
Dos monitos...
Un monito...

Cero monitos
Brincando en la cama,
Brincando en la cama,
La cama de la Mama.
Nadie se cayó y nadie se golpió.
Mamá lamó el doctor y él dijo,
"¿No hay dolor?"
Pues regresa esos monos a la cama,
¡Por favor!"

*Substitute monitos with changuitos depending upon how monkey is said among your Spanish speaking community.

** Say the word mama without the accent so that it rhymes with cama.

2

FIVE LITTLE MONKEYS JUMPING ON THE BED
Lesson Plan
By Silvia León

Age Group:
> 3 - 6 year olds

Materials Needed::
> Five Little Monkeys felt figures, a flannel board, large number cards (0 - 5), a gym mat, a play or real stethoscope, an apron and two telephones.

Objectives:
> After chanting the rhyme of the Five Little Monkeys several times, the children will:
>
> - memorize the rhyme
> - count the monkeys
> - find the numbers in the monkey's tails
> - practice the concept of subtraction
> - be introduced to the numeral zero
> - talk about their own bed

Procedure:

1) Place the felt bed figure on the flannel board. Ask the children if they can recognize what it is. Ask them if they have their own bed or share it with someone. What does it look like? (a bunk bed, a water bed, a sofa bed, etc.)

2) Have the children guess what animal you're going to place on the flannel board bed. Give them hints.

3) After the children have guessed correctly, ask them what they think these monkeys are going to do on the bed. Brainstorm answers.

4) Now place the monkeys on the flannel board and do the rhyme.

3

5) The second time around, let the children help you remove the fallen monkeys as you chant the rhyme together.

6) Repeat and add the hand motions. Use one hand, palms up, as the bed, and the other hand, open wide, as the five monkeys jumping. Twirl arms around for falling, touch and tilt head for bumping their heads, and use one hand on ear and the other by the mouth for the telephone.

7) Possible questions to ask the children:

How many monkeys are on the bed? How many have fallen?
How many were left on the bed at the end of the rhyme? (Make large number cards 0 - 5.) Show the number zero.
Who can find a hidden number in one of the monkey's tails?
Who can match this number card (1 - 5) to a monkey's tail?
Why did the mama call the doctor?
If you had been the doctor, what would you have recommended to the mama? Encourage creative answers.
Did the monkeys get hurt? Is it a good idea to jump on beds? Why or why not?

8) **Grand Finale!** Bring in a gym mat for a bed, 2 play telephones, a stethoscope, and an apron for the mama. Choose volunteers, and dramatize the Five Little Monkeys rhyme.

Related Literature:

Five Little Monkeys Jumping on the Bed, by Eileen Christelow
More Spaghetti I Say, by Rita Golden Gelman
Valentin, el Mono, by Tom Lafleur and Gale Bennan
Why Can't I Fly, by Rita Golden Gelman

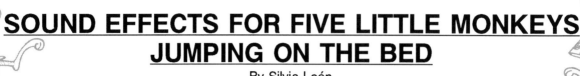

SOUND EFFECTS FOR FIVE LITTLE MONKEYS JUMPING ON THE BED

By Silvia León

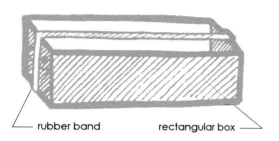

When the children say "...jumping on the bed" ("...brincando en la cama"), have several other children pluck the rubber band placed around a rectangular box for a jumping sound ... "boing, boing, boing"!

rubber band   rectangular box

Boing Boing Box

Give slide whistles to a couple of children to produce the falling sound effect in the part "one fell down" ("uno se cayó..."). Disinfect slide whistles with alcohol between children.

Slide Whistle

Have a child make a CRASH sound with the cymbals on the part "...and bumped his head" ("...y la cabeza se golpeó...").

Cymbals

Give 2 or 3 children hand bells for the telephone sound effect.

Hand Bells

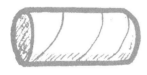

Give the part of Dr. Monkey to a child who will then talk through the toilet paper roll so that he sounds as if he were on the telephone when he says "No more monkeys ..." ("No más changos ...").

Toilet Paper Roll

MONKEYIN' AROUND THE MONKEY BARS

By Silvia León

Materials Needed:

- approximately 12 feet of paper or plastic vines and leaves
- a banana for each student
- horizontal bars

Procedure:

1) Hang paper or plastic vines and leaves over, under, and around the horizontal bars of your climbing equipment outdoors. To make paper vines, twirl green tissue paper into strands and then connect them together with tape. Now you have a vine! The children can help you make it. Next, tape heart shaped leaves to the vine.

2) String about 5 bananas at a time to the end of the horizontal bars.

3) Children will pretend to be monkeys, swinging across vines to catch their food. If you have a large class, provide other monkeyin' around activities as the children wait for their turn (jumping on a trampoline, walking, scratching, and making noises like a monkey, painting monkey faces on themselves, etc).

4) Help those children who aren't strong enough to make it across. Every "monkey" should get a banana as a reward for trying!

FIVE LITTLE SPECKLED FROGS

Traditional

C
Five little speckled frogs

F
Sat on a speckled log

C   G7
Eating a most delicious bug.

G7
Yum! Yum!

C
One jumped into the pool

F
Where it was nice and cool.

C   G7   C
Now there are four green speckled frogs.

C
Glub! Glub!

Four little speckled frogs...

Three little speckled frogs...

Two little speckled frogs...

One little speckled frog...

...Now there are no more speckled frogs!

Glub! Glug! Glub!

CINCO RANITAS

Translation by Silvia León

C
Cinco ranitas
F
Con muchas manchitas
C   G7
Sentadas arriba de un tronco.
G7
¡Cro! ¡Cro!
C
Una rana cayó
F
Adentro de un lago.
C G7   C
Ahora quedan cuatro ranas.
C
¡Cro! ¡Cro!

Cuatro ranitas...

Tres ranitas...

Dos ranitas...

Una ranita...

...Ahora no quedan más ranas.

¡Cro! ¡Cro! ¡Cro!

FIVE LITTLE SPECKLED FROGS
Lesson Plan
By Silvia León

Age Group:
3 - 6 year olds

Materials Needed:
Five Little Speckled Frogs flannel board figures, a flannel board, a large blue sheet or piece of cloth, 5 green poster boards, 5 crates or chairs.

Objectives:
After singing the Five Little Speckled Frogs several times, the children will:

- memorize the song
- practice counting to 5
- practice the concept of subtraction
- understand the definition of speckled
- state the name of different bugs
- have a better understanding of a frog's habitat, movements, sounds and diet.

Procedure:

1) Place the pond felt piece on the flannel board. Ask the children to identify what they see and try to guess what animal you are going to place on it. Give them hints!

2) Have the children count the frogs together with you as you place them on the flannel board.

3) Tell the children that today you will teach them a song about these five little frogs. Sing the song and repeat.

4) Ask the children what they think the word speckled means. Brainstorm creative answers.

5) After each verse, ask the children how many frogs are left on the log. How many have jumped in the pool?

6) Other possible questions to ask the children:

What sounds do frogs make?
How do frogs move?
Why did they jump into the pool?
What do frogs like to eat? (insects)
How many different insects can you find and name?
(ant, bee, caterpillar, ladybug, fly, cricket, dragonfly, mosquito)
How do frogs catch their food? (with tongue)
Where do frogs live? (almost anywhere but mostly in damp places like ponds or trees)
If you were a frog, what would you eat? How would you move, talk to your frog friends or catch your food?
Accept all answers.

7) **Grand Finale!** Make five large frogs from green poster boards. Cut out an opening for children's faces. Lay out a blue sheet or piece of cloth on the floor over your classroom rug. Place chairs or up-side-down crates on top of the blue sheet as the log. Now the children can act out the song. They can either sit or squat on the crates and jump into the "pool" (blue sheet) when it's their turn.

Related Literature:
The Boastful Bullfrog by Keith Faulkner
El Sapo Distraido by Marcela Cabrera
Frog Went-A-Courtin' by John Langstaff
Jump, Frog, Jump by Robert Kalan
Las Manchas del Sapo by Marjorie E. Herrman
The Story of the Dancing Frog by Quentin Blake

FROG MOVEMENT ACTIVITY

By Silvia León

Materials Needed:

- masking tape
- a "boing, boing" box (see page 5)
- frog music

Procedure:

1) Make large lily pads (circles) of about 12" in diameter on your classroom rug using masking tape. Make enough lily pads for each of your students.

2) After discussing, reading, and singing about frogs, have the children pretend to be frogs, jumping from lily pad to lily pad. Whenever they hear you pluck your "boing-boing" box, they are to jump around like frogs. Whenever you stop, they can make buzzing sounds and pretend to be catching and eating delicious, juicy bugs! Encourage unique jumps and bug-eating pantomimes.

3) You may also want to play some type of bouncy frog music. The book <u>Artsplay</u>, by Leon Burton and Kathy Kuroda has frog music as well as many other types of creative songs and movement activities. The book contains small floppy records that are stored on the back of the front cover.

FROG SOUND GUIRO
by Silvia León

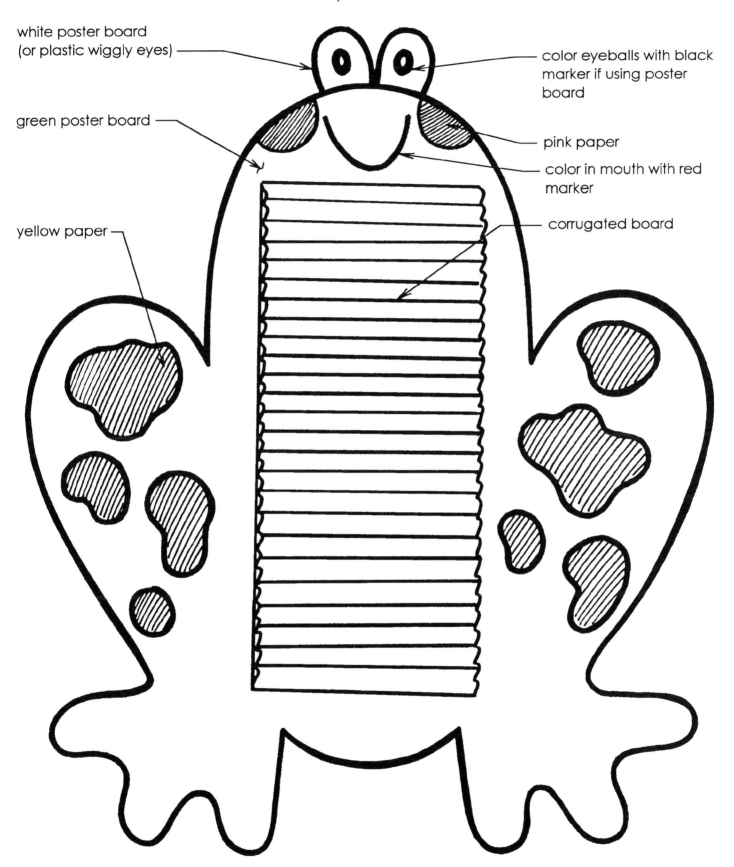

white poster board
(or plastic wiggly eyes)

color eyeballs with black
marker if using poster
board

green poster board

pink paper

color in mouth with red
marker

corrugated board

yellow paper

<u>Note:</u> Laminate frog before attaching the corrugated board. This will aid in the replacement of the corrugated board when it has gone flat. Use a popscicle stick to scrape the board making frog croaking sounds.

12

FIVE LITTLE PUMPKINS

traditional

Five little pumpkins sitting on a gate,

The first one said, "My it's getting late."

The second one said, "There are witches in the air!"

The third one said, "I don't care!"

The fourth one said, "Let's run! Let's run!"

The fifth one said, "It's only Halloween fun."

Then OOOOOOO went the wind.

And **OUT** went the lights!

And the five little pumpkins ran clear out of sight!

CINCO CALABACITAS

translated by Silvia León

Cinco calabacitas en la reja sentaditas,

La primera dijo, "¡Se está haciendo tarde!"

La segunda dijo, "¡Hay brujas en el aire!"

La tercera dijo, "No me importa a mí."

La cuarta dijo, "¡Vámonos de aquí!"

La quinta dijo, "Es solo Halloween."

Entonces UUUUUUU sopló el viento.

Y **PUF** las luces se apagaron!

Y las cinco calabacitas corrieron porque se

asustaron!

FIVE LITTLE PUMPKINS
Lesson Plan
By Silvia León

Age Group:
   3 - 6 year olds

Materials Needed:
   Five Little Pumpkins felt figures, a flannel board, five orange poster boards and five crates.

Objectives:
   After chanting the rhyme of the Five Little Pumpkins several times the children will:

- memorize the rhyme
- count pumpkins
- be introduced to the concept of first, second, third, etc.
- discuss the various sizes and shapes of pumpkins
- verbalize about the facial expressions of the pumpkins and the emotions they depict
- share their own feelings arising from different situations
- identify the rhyming words in the poem (for older students)

Procedure:
   1) Place the felt figures of the gate and the witch on the flannel board.

   2) Tell the children that something is going to sit on the gate. Brainstorm as to what it may be. Give them hints, "It is round, it's a vegetable, it's orange, etc."

   3) Tell the rhyme using different voice intonations to go with the facial expressions of the pumpkins. For example, use a sleepy voice for the first, a shaky voice for the second, an angry voice for the third, an excited voice for the fourth and a silly voice for the fifth pumpkin.

4)   Have your teacher assistant or an adult volunteer stand next to the classroom lights. When the rhyme says, "... and OUT went the lights," have an adult turn off the classroom lights. Sit those children who may be frightened of the dark next to you.

5)   Repeat the rhyme. This time have the children help you place the felt figures on the flannel board and turn off the lights.

6)   Ask questions:

> How many pumpkins are on the gate?
> Which is the biggest pumpkin? The smallest? The same size as another one? Etc...
> Where did they come from?
> Why did they leave?
> What did the first one say? The second one? Etc...
> How did the third pumpkin feel? The fifth one? Etc...
> When I say a certain word, you tell me another word from the poem that rhymes with it.
> If you could be one of the pumpkins on the gate, which one would you be? Why?

7)   **Grand Finale!** Make 5 large pumpkins from orange poster boards and cut out the center for the children's faces. Have the children dramatize the rhyme. Use up-side-down crates as the gate.

Related Literature:

Big Pumpkin, by Erica Silverman
Pumpkin, Pumpkin, by Jeanne Titherington
The Little Old Lady Who Was Not Afraid of Anything, by Linda Williams
The Pumpkin Blanket, by Deborah Turney Zagwyn

PAPER BAG PUMPKIN PATCH

By Silvia León

Materials Needed:

- brown paper bags (different sizes)
- newspaper
- poster paint (all colors)
- paint brushes
- paint cups
- tongue depressors
- green construction paper
- green pipe cleaners
- a variety of 3-dimensional objects (buttons, feathers, etc.)
- bales of hay (optional)

Procedure:

1) Ask your students to bring brown paper bags from home. A variety of sizes is preferable because pumpkins do come in various sizes!

2) The children will stuff their paper bags with newspapers leaving 1/4 of the top part of the bag empty.

3) Have your students twist the top part of the bag shut. This will make a stem-like shape. You may need masking tape to keep bigger and thicker paper bags closed.

4) Give each student an empty paint cup and let them mix their own orange. Demonstrate beforehand using approximately 2 fingers of yellow paint with 1 squirt of red. Stir with tongue depressor. A variety of shades of orange will be created . . . just like real pumpkins! Paint the stem either green or brown.

5) Trace each student's hand and have an adult volunteer cut it out. This will be the pumpkin's leaf. Glue to the stem. Twirl a green pipe cleaner around a pencil and then twist around the stem to give the appearance of a vine.

6) Now comes the creative, fun part! Let your children paint funny faces on their pumpkins with other colors of paint. Provide 3-dimensional objects such as buttons, feathers, colored macaroni, etc. for additional texture and interest. Let your children go! Remember that the process (the fun in doing it) is more important than what the end results look like.

7) Bring bales of hay into your classroom and make your own paper bag pumpkin patch! (This is optional but creates a terrific display for the children's pumpkins.)

PUMPKIN SEED BAG TOSS

By Silvia León

4' x 5' x 12" plywood board

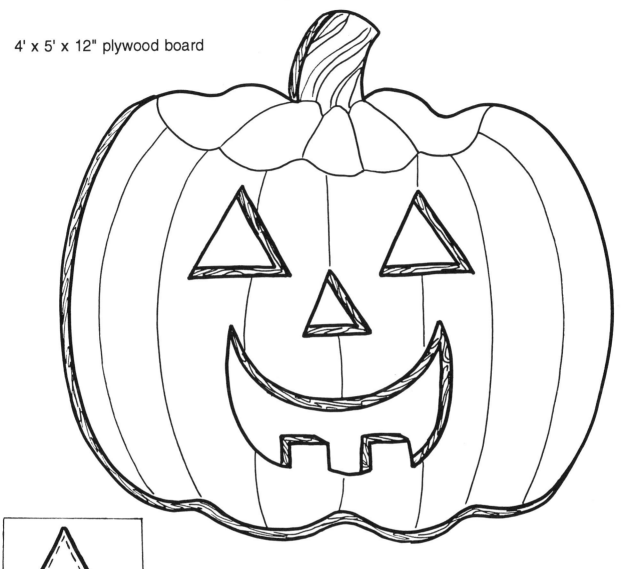

5" x 8" of sturdy
pale yellow fabric.
Enlarge the drawing
on a copy machine

1) Photocopy the pumpkin drawing onto clear acetate

2) On an overhead projector, use the clear acetate copy of the pumpkin and draw the image onto a piece of 4' x 5' plywood board.

3) Ask a parent volunteer who is handy in carpentry to cut out for you the pumpkin shape, eyes, nose, and mouth you drew on the plywood. Paint the pumpkin orange with a green or brown stem.

4) Ask another parent volunteer to make you 15 bean bags in the shape of pumpkin seeds. Stuff with beans or rice.

BABY CHICKS

(Translation by unknown author)

A   D
　Baby chicks are crying, "Pio, pio, pio!"
D   A   E   A
Mama we are hungry, Mama we are cold."

A   D   A
Mama brings them wheat. Mama brings them corn.
D   A   E   A
She will feed them dinner. She will keep them warm.

A   D   A
Under her two wings, she cuddles them and sings,
D   A   E   A
"No more time for play, sleep until next day."

A   D   A
Early in the morning when the sun is shining,
D   A   E   A
Behind Daddy Rooster, baby chicks go running.

A   D   A
Then they tell their mommy, "Pio, pio, pio!
D   A   E   A
Mama we are hungry, Mama we are cold."

19

LOS POLLITOS

(Traditional)

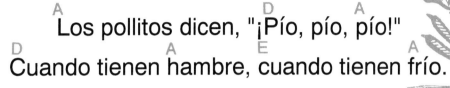

    A   D   A
Los pollitos dicen, "¡Pío, pío, pío!"
D   A   E   A
Cuando tienen hambre, cuando tienen frío.

    A   D   A
La gallina busca el maíz y el trigo,
D   A   E   A
Les da de comer y les busca abrigo.

    A   D   A
Bajo sus dos alas acurrucaditos,
D   A   E   A
Hasta el otro día duermen los pollitos.

A   D   A
Cuando el sol envía sus primeros rayos,
D   A   E   A
Los pollitos salen detráz de Don Gallo.

A   D   A
Vuelven los pollitos temblando de frío,
D   A   E   A
Y siguen diciendo, "Pio, pio, pio."

BABY CHICKS
Lesson Plan
By Silvia León

Age Group:

   3 - 6 year olds

Materials Needed:

   Baby Chicks felt figures, a flannel board, The Chicken Song or any other song with a fun beat?

Objective:

   After singing the song Baby Chicks several times and talking about it, the children will:

   - identify the chicks, hen and rooster as a family
   - imitate the cry of a baby chick
   - imitate the sounds of a hen and a rooster
   - understand the origin of a chick
   - understand that a chick's cry, like a human baby's cry communicates a need to its mommy
   - understand the difference between hens and roosters
   - pretend to move like hens or roosters to the Chicken Song

Procedure:

   1)   Place the Baby Chick felt figures on the flannel board. Ask the children to identify the animals they see.

   2)   Ask questions:

   Where do baby chicks come from?
   How do they get out of the egg?
   Where do eggs come from:
   What sound does a hen make?
   If the hen is a chick's mommy, what farm animal is the chick's daddy? What sound does he make?
   What sounds to baby chicks make?
   What are they trying to say to their mommy?
   What sounds do human babies make?

What are they trying to say to their mommy?

3) Tell the boys and girls that today you will teach them a song about baby chicks who cry to their mommy because they need certain things. Ask them to listen carefully.

4) Sing the song. Repeat.

5) Ask the children why the baby chicks cried? What did their mommy do?

6) Sing the song again and let the children join in.

7) **Grand Finale!** Pretend to be chicks inside an egg.(You may want to supplement this part by either presenting pictures of chicks still in their eggs, movies or books dealing with the subject or by actually hatching eggs from an incubator in your own classroom.) Guide the children through the process. "How would your body be inside an egg? Is it dark? Are you cramped? How does it feel being inside an egg? How are you going to get out?" Pantomime hatching and moving like a new chick. Now the chick gets older and bigger. Ask the children, "Who will grow up to be hens and who will be roosters? Why?" Move around the classroom and make sounds like a hen or rooster. Play the Chicken Song. If you know the hand and body motions to this particular song, simplify the movements. Have a great time!

Related Literature:

Across the Steam, by Nancy Tafuri
Chicken and Egg, by Christine Back and Jens Olesen
Henny Penny, by H. Werner Zimmermann (available in Spanish)
La Pollita Vivita, by Janet Hillman (available in English)
The Little Red Hen, by Lucinda McQueen (available in Spanish)
Pollito Pequeñito Cuenta Hasta Diez, by Margaret Friskey & Katherine Evans
Rosie's Walk, by Pat Hutchins

LOS POLLITOS COLOR MATCHING GAME

By Silvia León

Object of the game:

To match pom pom chicks to an egg of the same color.

Materials needed:

- 2 large pom poms of the same color in a variety of colors
- large plastic Easter eggs, in a variety of colors
- orange pipecleaners
- plastic moving eyes
- orange and pink felt
- hot glue

Directions:

1) Hot glue pompoms of the same color together.

2) Cut out felt beaks (orange felt) and cheeks (pink felt).

3) Hot glue eyes, beaks, and cheeks to chick head.

4) Cut orange pipecleaners about 2-1/2 inches long (2 for each chick) for legs.

5) Cut orange pipecleaners about 2 inches long (2 for each chick) for feet.

6) Twist the smaller piece of pipecleaner around the larger one to give the shape of chicken feet...somewhat!

7) Hot glue feet to bottom pom pom.

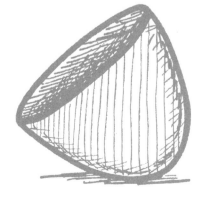

beak pattern

cheek pattern

23

RAINBOW EGG PUZZLES
By Silvia León

Materials Needed:

- sturdy oval paper plates
- pre-cut tissue paper in a variety of shapes and colors
- glue
- water
- flat bristle paint brushes
- paint cups
- scissors
- spray varnish
- large box

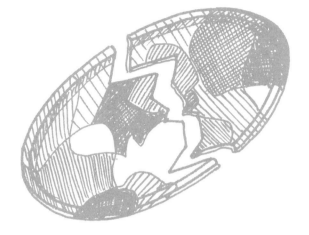

Procedure:

1) Dilute glue with water to the consistency of paint.

2) Pour diluted glue into paint cups.

3) Give a sturdy oval paper plate to each child. Demonstrate how to glue the tissue paper onto the plate. Encourage overlapping of different colors to create new ones.

4) When the children have completely covered their plates with tissue paper and claim to be finished, set them outdoors to dry.

5) When they have completely dried, cover the plates with spray varnish for a glossy look.

6) Have an adult cut the plates in half making irregular, puzzle-like shapes.

7) Put all the plate halves in a large box for children to match on the rug during free-play time.

SIX LITTLE DUCKS

author unknown

Six little ducks that I once knew. (F) (C7)

Fat ones, skinny ones, fair ones too, (F)

But the one little duck with the feather on his back, (C7)

He led the others with his quack, quack, quack, (F)

Quack, quack, quack, . . . quack, quack, quack, (C7)

He led the others with his quack, quack, quack. (F)

Down by the river they would go, (F) (C7)

Wibble-wobble, wibble-wobble to and fro. (F)

But the one little duck with the feather on his back, (C7)

He led the others with his quack, quack, quack, (F)

Quack, quack, quack, . . . quack, quack, quack, (C7)

He led the others with his quack, quack, quack! (F)

Back from the river they would come, (F) (C7)

Wibble-wobble, wibble-wobble, ho, hum, hum. (F)

But the one little duck with the feather on his back, (C7)

He led the others with his quack, quack, quack, (F)

Quack, quack, quack, . . . quack, quack, quack, (C7)

He led the others with his quack, quack, quack! (F)

SEIS PATITOS

translation by Silvia León

F   C₇
Seis patitos* que conocí

F
Flacos, gordos y amarillos yo los ví.

          C₇
Pero el patito con la colita de pluma

          F
Guíaba a los otros con su cuá, cuá, cuá,

        C₇
Cuá, cuá, cuá, . . . cuá, cuá, cuá,

         F
Guíaba a los otros con su cuá, cuá, cuá.

    F   C₇
Iban al río a nadar

          F
Bailaban y bailaban con su cha-cha-cha.

          C₇
Pero el patito con la colita de pluma

         F
Guíaba a los otros con su cuá, cuá, cuá,

        C₇
Cuá, cuá, cuá, . . . cuá, cuá, cuá,

         F
Guíaba a los otros con su cuá, cuá, cuá!

   F   C₇
Los patitos regresaron,

         F
Tambaleando, tambaleando, mojados.

         C₇
Pero el patito con la colita de pluma

         F
Guíaba a los otros con su cuá, cuá, cuá,

        C₇
Cuá, cuá, cuá, . . . cuá, cuá, cuá,

         F
Guíaba a los otros con su cuá, cuá, cuá!

* Substitute paticos for patitos depending on how the word is used among your Spanish-speaking community.

SIX LITTLE DUCKS
Lesson Plan
By Silvia León

Age Group:
   3 - 6 year olds

Materials Needed:
   Six Little Ducks felt figures, a flannel board, a large paper or ostrich feather, classroom musical instruments.

Objective:
   After singing, discussing and dramatizing the song "Six Little Ducks, the children will:

   • practice counting to six
   • imitate loud and soft duck sounds
   • imitate fast and slow duck movements
   • identify similarities and differences among the ducks
   • be introduced to 5 musical instruments: maracas, xylophone, triangle, tambourine and cymbals
   • identify position of ducks as either first, last or in the middle
   • understand that ducks lay eggs, have feathers and belong to the bird family
   • understand that ducks can either travel on land, water, or in the air

Procedure:

   1)   Place the Six Little Ducks felt figures on the flannel board and tell the children that today they will learn a song about six little ducks. Count the ducks together.

   2)   Sing the song. Repeat and allow children to join in whenever they feel ready.

   3)   Ask children to imitate the sounds that the ducks made in the song. If a duck was very far away, how would his quack sound? If he were next to you, how would he sound?

4) Imitate different duck movements. Guide them through a pretend road, waddling, then running down a hill to a pond where they swim and finally fly away. Point out that ducks can travel by walking, running, swimming or flying. How many ways can people travel?

5) Tell the children that ducks belong to the bird family. All animals of the bird family lay eggs and have feathers. Ducks lay eggs and have feathers; therefore, they belong to the bird family. Ask the children if they can think of other animals that lay eggs and have feathers.

6) Have the children look at the Six Little Ducks felt figures. How are they alike and how are they different? Point out how ducks have different shapes and colored feathers just as people have different shapes, skin and hair color.

7) Ask the children which duck is first in line. Which one is last? Which one is in the middle? Now change the position of the ducks and repeat the questions.

8) Ask the children to name the different musical instruments the ducks are playing. Have children find matching musical instruments from those displayed in the music center of your classroom.

9) **Grand Finale!** Choose one child as the leader and pin a large paper or ostrich feather on his back. Have each child select a musical instrument of his choice from your music center. Now have a duck parade around the playground. Encourage your children to play their instruments softly, then loudly, slowly, then fast.

Related Literature:
Chickens Aren't the Only Ones. by Ruth Heller
Five Little Ducks, by Raffi - Raffi Songs to Read
Has Visto a Mi Patito?, by Nancy Tafuri (available in English)
Petunia, by Roger Duvoisin
Ten Little Ducks, by Franklin Hammond
The Ugly Duckling, by Brenda Parkes and Judith Smith (available in Spanish)

CHA-CHA-CHA PAINT BOTTLE MARACAS

By Silvia León

Soak your empty paint bottles in a bucket of water and liquid detergent overnight. Give to a parent volunteer to scrub clean. After they have dried, glue construction paper around the bottle and give to your students to decorate with markers, feathers, macaroni, seashells, etc. Fill half-way with either beans, rice, sand, small pebbles, etc., and . . . VOILA!! You have recycled paint bottles into *b-e-a-u-t-i-f-u-l* maracas!!

Find a spicy cha-cha-cha song (the soundtrack from the movie Mambo Kings has terrific selections). Have your students dance free-style as they play their maracas to the Latin beat!

FEATHER DUSTER MURAL

By Silvia León

Materials Needed:

- White butcher paper
- 8 small plastic buckets
- 8 feather dusters
- 8 different colors of tempera paint
- newspaper
- adult & child smocks
- dishwashing liquid or starch

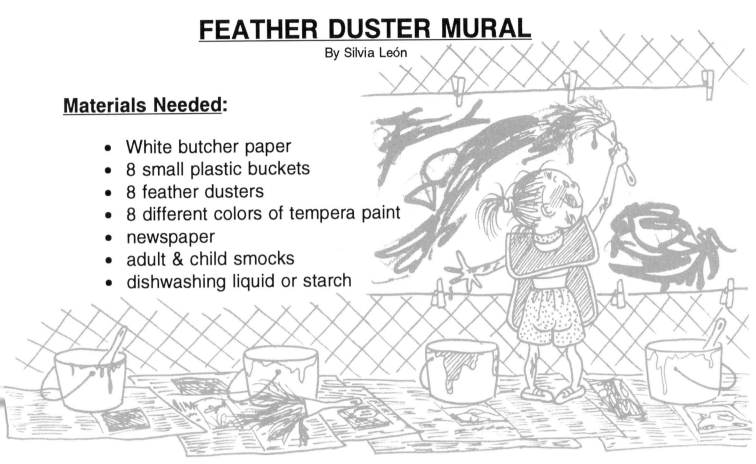

Procedure:

1) Tape a long piece of butcher paper (at least 12 feet) to your school fence or outdoor wall.

2) In 8 small plastic buckets pour paint and dilute with water to the consistency of a milk shake. Add a squirt of liquid detergent or starch. This will aid in the clean-up and washing of little fingers.

3) Spread newspapers under the butcher paper. Place the buckets on the newspaper with a feather duster in each bucket.

4) Make sure your blooming feather-duster-artists, as well as you, wear smocks. This is a messy activity but too much fun to pass up. Invite parent volunteers to help.

5) Let your children overlap and mix colors if they wish. Save the mural and use as a background for your bulletin boards.

TEN LITTLE CHILDREN

By Silvia León

(Sung to the tune of the Ten Little Indians)

F
One little, two little, three little children,
C₇
Four little, five little, six little children,
F
Seven little, eight little, nine little children
C₇   F
Ten little happy kids.

Now wiggle your fingers
And wiggle your toes...
Ten little happy kids.

Stretch up big
And get down small...
Ten little happy kids.

Now jump and jump
And jump so high...
Ten little happy kids.

DIÉZ NIÑITOS

By Silvia León

(Cantado a la melodía de los Diéz Inditos)

F
Uno, dos y tres niñitos,
C₇
Cuatro, cinco, seis niñitos,
F
Siete, ocho, nueve niñitos,
C₇   F
Diéz niñitos son.

Muevan sus deditos
De las manos y pies...
Diéz niñitos son.

Estirense grandes
Y ponganse chiquitos...
Diéz niñitos son.

Brinquen y brinquen
Y brinquen muy alto...
Diéz niñitos son.

TEN LITTLE CHILDREN
Lesson Plan
By Silvia León

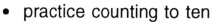

Age Group:
3 - 6 year olds

Materials Needed:
Ten Little Children felt figures, large numerals (1-10) approximately 8" X 11" in size and two or three pieces of different colored roving or yarn, 8 feet in length.

Objectives:
After discussing about and singing the Ten Little Children song several times the children will:

- practice counting to ten
- practice arranging numbers from one to ten
- practice identifying numbers from one to ten
- point out similarities and differences among the Ten Little Children
- point out similarities and differences among themselves and other children
- have a better understanding and appreciation of their own identity
- have a better understanding and appreciation of other races and of people with special needs
- practice counting to ten in sign language

Special Note to Teachers:

The following plans, although very simple, should be divided into several days because in-depth discussions and feelings will surface when talking about differences among people. Use your own judgment and let the children's attention span guide you as to how much or how little you will present on any given day. You will find suggested places to stop in the lesson plan.

Procedure:

1) Tell the boys and girls that today they will learn a song about ten little children.

2) As you sing the song, place the Ten Little Children figures, one by one on your flannel board.

3) Repeat and allow the children to join in the song whenever they want to.

4) Ask volunteers to point out and name the numerals they see.

5) Scramble the Ten Little Children on the flannel board and have children help you arrange them in numerical, sequential order.

6) Give large numbers to ten volunteers and have them stand up or hold up their number when they hear it sung. (For older children, scramble the volunteers and let them find their places in numerical order.)

* **(This is a good ending point. You may want to continue the following plans on another day.)**

7) Ask children to look closely at the Ten Little Children on the flannel board. How are they the same? Make sets of children with the felt figures. For example, place the children who have black hair on one side of the flannel board and those who do not on the other side, etc.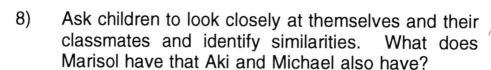

8) Ask children to look closely at themselves and their classmates and identify similarities. What does Marisol have that Aki and Michael also have?

9) Make large circles on the floor with different colored roving or yarn and have children that have similar attributes stand inside them. Let children make up the rule. For example, a child will direct those with red socks to stand inside the blue circle and those whose socks are not red stand in the yellow circle.

* **(Here is another spot where you might want to stop and continue on another day.)**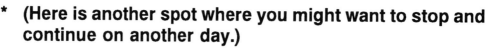

10) Discuss the differences children see among the Ten Little Children felt figures.

11) Have children look at themselves and their classmate and find differences.

12) Ask children how they feel about people who have different skin tones, shapes and sizes. Their answers will give you a good indication about misconceptions, attitudes and prejudices they might already have. Discuss and allow them to ask you many questions!

13) Talk about people with special needs. Again, ask them how they feel when they see someone in a wheelchair or someone who is blind. Can a person with special needs be a mom, have a job, go to school?

14) Emphasize how all people are the same yet very different. Being unique is what makes us the special persons we are ... a one-of-a-kind, like a work of art!

15) **Grand Finale!** Look at the Ten Little Children very closely and notice that they are counting in sign language. Show the children how to sign from one to ten. (See drawings on page 37.) Practice a few times. Now try signing as you sing the song.

Related Literature:

Here Are My Hands, by Bill Martin and John Archambault
I Like Me, by Barbara J. Neasi
The Land of Many Colors, by the Klamath County YMCA Family Preschool
The Rhythm Eco, by Kathy Poelker (available in Spanish)
We Are All Alike ... We Are All Different, by the Kindergartners at Cheltenham Elementary School

COUNTING TO TEN IN
AMERICAN SIGN LANGUAGE

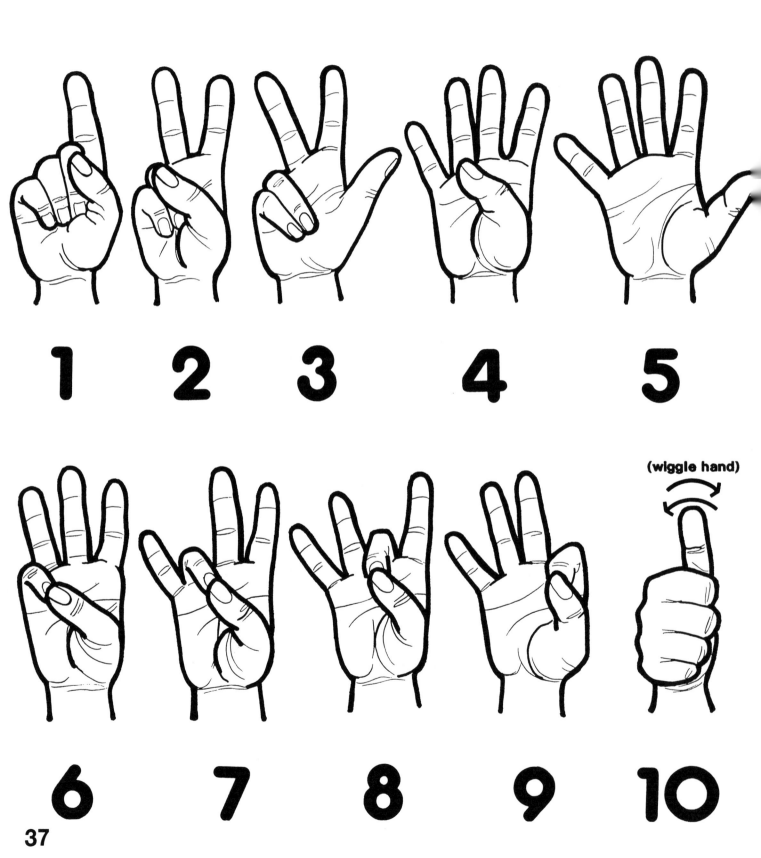

1   2   3   4   5

(wiggle hand)

6   7   8   9   10

HAPPY HANDPRINTS
By Silvia León

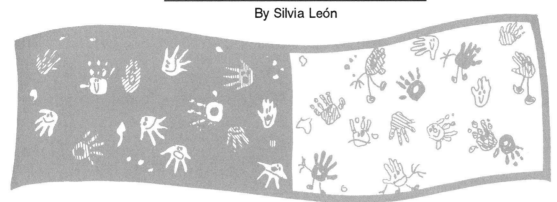

Materials Needed:
- tempera paint in different skin tones
- large sponges
- paper plates
- black butcher paper
- white butcher paper
- color markers
- plastic wiggly eyes

Procedure:
1) Mix or buy people color skin tone paints.

2) Pour the different paints over large sponges on paper plates.

3) Allow children to press their hands on the sponges and arbitrarily print their hands on a long piece of black butcher paper. Encourage creative ways to print hands (fingerprints, side of hand, overlapping hands, etc.). Let children print as many hands as they want. Don't worry about cleaning hands. After using one color, they can paint right over their hands with another color.

4) The next day, repeat the activity on white butcher paper. This will demonstrate to the children that no one has pure black nor pure white skin.

5) After the handprints have dried, children can draw faces on them with different colored markers and attach plastic wiggly eyes.

FIVE LITTLE MONKEYS
SITTING IN A TREE

Traditional

Five little monkeys sitting in a tree

Teasing Mr. Crocodile,

"You can't catch me! You can't catch me!"

Well along comes Mr. Crocodile

Just as quiet as can be...

And he SNATCHED that monkey

Right out of the tree!

Four little monkeys...

Three little monkeys...

Two little monkeys...

One little monkey...

No more monkeys sitting in a tree

Teasing Mr. Crocodile,

"You can't catch me! You can't catch me!"

Well along comes Mr. Crocodile

Just as quiet as can be

And he looked... And he looked...

And he went back home

Just as FULL as he could be!

CINCO MONITOS
SENTADOS EN EL ARBOL

Translation by Silvia León

Un día por el río un cocodrilo nadó.

Miró para arriba y cinco *monos vió.

Se burlaban y reían,

"¡No me agarras a mí

Con tus dientes y tu lengüa

Y tu grande nariz!"

Calladito, calladito el cocodrilo nadó,

Cuando...¡GLUP!...al pobre mono

se lo comió.

Un día por el río un cocodrilo nadó.

Miró para arriba y cuatro monos vió...

Un día por el río un cocodrilo nadó.

¡Miró para arriba y a NADIE vió!

Calladito, calladito el cocodrilo nadó

Y con su panza** MUY llena se regresó.

*Substitute monitos with chanquitos depending upon how monkey is said among our Spanish speaking community.

** Substitute the word panza with barriga, depending upon how your Spanish-speaking community uses the term for an animal's stomach

FIVE LITTLE MONKEYS SITTING IN A TREE
Lesson Plan
by Silvia León

Age Group:

3 - 6 year olds

Materials Needed:

Five Little Monkeys (sitting on a tree) felt figures, a flannel board, chart paper and a marker.

Objectives:

After chanting and discussing the Five Little Monkeys (sitting in a tree) rhyme, the children will:

- practice counting monkeys
- find the hidden numbers (1-5) in the monkey tails
- count the bananas each monkey carries
- practice the concept of subtraction
- give creative responses to questions
- identify possible locations where monkeys and crocodiles may be found
- move like a monkey through a make-believe jungle
- make creative sounds of objects found in the make-believe jungle

Procedures:

1) Place the felt figures on the flannel board. Ask the children to identify the animals they see.

2) Count together the monkeys on the tree. Look for the hidden numbers in their tails. "How many bananas is the monkey with the number one tail holding? How about the monkey with the number two tail?" Etc...

3) Tell the boys and girls that today they will learn a rhyme about the five little monkeys they see on the flannel board.

4) Chant the rhyme. Use hand motions. Repeat.

5) Allow children to subtract monkeys off the flannel board as you repeat the rhyme together once more. As each monkey is eaten, ask how many are left on the tree?

6) Ask questions and chart the children's responses:

> Where can people find monkeys and crocodiles?
> Where do you think this rhyme takes place? (a farm, a city, a beach, a zoo, a jungle) Why?
> Where did the crocodile come from? Keep asking, "Where else could he have come from?" until all possibilities have been exhausted. Accept all answers. This forces children to think creatively.
> Why did the crocodile eat the monkeys?
> How do you think the crocodile was able to grab the monkeys who were up in the tree? Brainstorm for creative answers.
> If you were a monkey, would you tease a crocodile? Why or why not?
> Read the answers back to your students. Children will see the relationship of the spoken to the printed word.

7) **Grand Finale!** Go on a Crocodile Safari! (Similar to the Bear Hunt.) Pretend to be monkeys. Use body movements and creative sound effects as you travel through the jungle. Swing from branches, climb down tree trunks, step on crunchy leaves, swish through tall grass, squish over quicksand, climb a hill, swim across a river, tip-toe on the sandy shore where the crocodile lays sleeping. Describe what he looks like but remember to whisper so that he doesn't ...oops! Too late! He woke up and is now chasing YOU! Reverse your motions. Once you climb the tree, you'll be safe again!

Related Literature:

Caps for Sale, by Esphyr Slobodkina
Cuento de un Cocodrilo, by Jose and Ariane Aruego (available in English)
Curious George, by H. A. Rey
Five Little Monkeys Sitting in a Tree, by Eileen Christelow
Little Gorilla, by Ruth Borstein

MONKEY TAIL PRINTS

By Silvia León

Materials Needed:

- thick pieces of cardboard (one per student of approx. 5 X 8 inches)
- thick string, rope or cord
- glue
- tempera paint
- white art or construction paper

Procedure:

1) Show your children pictures of monkey tails. Point out how it changes shapes as it moves.

2) Give each child a piece of rope, cord or thick string of approximately 12 inches. Show them how to make swirls and "S" shapes. Let them play, making different shapes on the floor. Tell them that they are making " monkey tails!"

3) Next, show your class how to make monkey tail prints:

Have the children glue the cord in whatever shape they'd like onto a thick piece of cardboard.

Save until the following day to allow for the glue to completely dry.

The children select whatever color of paint they'd like and with a paintbrush will apply it onto the cord. Each child chooses one color and then they can trade their tail design with a friend if they'd like. This will allow children to add other shapes and colors to their paper. However, the child may also choose to keep one design and color, repeating the print throughout his paper. Let them also choose the color of construction paper they'd like or white art paper.

The patterns that will result will make you go "ape" over prints!

EAT A CHOCOLATE MONKEY

By Silvia León

Ingredients:

- 1 gallon of chocolate ice cream
- 1 package of vanilla wafer cookies
- 1 large box of raisins
- 1 package of thin red licorice, cut into 1 1/2" lengths
- 1 package of shredded coconut
- paper plate for each student
- ice cream scooper

Directions:

The children will:

1) Scoop out a ball of chocolate ice cream onto a plate.

2) Sink a vanilla wafer on each side of the ice cream ball as ears.

3) Insert raisin eyes and nose.

4) Add red licorice for mouth.

5) Place shredded coconut on top of ice cream head for hair.

6) Pretend to be crocodiles eating up a monkey. Yummy!

THE EENCY WEENCY SPIDER

Traditional

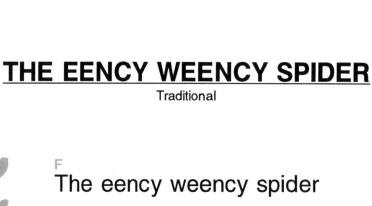

F
The eency weency spider

C   F
Went up the water spout.

Down came the rain

C   F
And washed the spider out!

Out came the sun

C   F
And dried up all the rain.

And the eency weency spider

C   F
Went up the spout again.

THE GREAT BIG SPIDER . . .

The teeny weeny spider . . .

45

LA ARAÑA PEQUEÑITA

Translation by Silvia León

F
La araña pequeñita
C   F
Subió por el drenaje.

Vino la lluvia
C   F
Y se la llevó!

Salió el sol
C   F
Y todo lo secó.

Y la araña pequeñita
C   F
Subió y subió y subió.

LA ARAÑA BIEN GRANDOTA . . .

La araña chirriquitita . . .

46

THE EENCY WEENCY SPIDER
Lesson Plan
By Silvia León

Age Group:
3 - 6 year olds

Materials Needed:
The Eency Weency Spider felt figures, a flannel board and poster boards in the shape of a water spout, cloud, sun and spiders (optional).

Objectives:
After discussing and singing the song several times the children will:

- share with the class about their own personal encounters with spiders
- use a low or a high pitch voice to differentiate the sizes of the spiders
- identify the difference between small, medium and large
- move fingers or body to correspond with the spider's size
- have a better understanding of a spider's anatomy
- understand the meaning and function of a water spout
- respond creatively to open-ended questions

Procedures:
1) Ask the boys and girls if they have ever seen a real spider. "Where? What did it look like? How did you feel? What did you do?"

2) Tell the children that today they will learn a song about a spider called The Eency Weency Spider. "What does eency weency mean?"

3) Place the house with the water spout on the flannel board. As you sing the song move the medium sized spider up the water spout. When singing, "Down came the rain..." place the cloud on the flannel board and slide the spider down. Finally, when you sing, "Out came the sun..." take off the cloud, introduce the sun and have the spider climb the water spout again.

4) Repeat the song. Have a helper manipulate the felt figures on the flannel board.

5) This time as you sing the song, show the children the hand motions.

6) Now tell the boys and girls that the eency weency spider has a cousin who is a GREAT BIG SPIDER. Bring out the largest spider and in your deepest, lowest voice sing the song again. Exaggerate your hand and arm motions to portray a huge spider.

7) Tell the child that this GREAT BIG SPIDER is married to a teeny weeny spider. Bring out the smallest spider. Repeat the song using your highest pitched voice. Use only your fingers for the motions.

8) Ask the children:

Which way was the spider going? (up)
Where was he going? Brainstorm for creative answers.
What made him fall down?
What did the sun do?
Which spider is the largest, smallest, medium?
If spiders could talk how would the GREAT BIG SPIDER say "hello"? How about the teeny weeny spider?
How many legs do spiders have? Do spiders' legs come out of their body or out of their head? (head) Where do your legs come out of, your body or your head? (Check the children's heads to make sure no one has a leg sticking out. The children find this concept to be very funny!)
Why do spiders have legs on their head? Brainstorm for creative answers. How many eyes do spiders have? (eight) How many eyes do you have? Why do spiders need so many eyes? Brainstorm for creative answers. What do you think would happen if people had eight eyes and eight legs on their heads?

9) Go outdoors and look for a real water spout. "What's a water spout used for?" (Collects rain on the roof and drains the water down to the ground.) Look around the water spout for spiders and spider webs.

10) **Grand Finale!** Dramatize the Eency Weency Spider song. Out of poster boards make a large water spout, cloud, sun and three different size spiders. Cut an oval opening in the middle for the children's faces. (This is optional. Children do not necessarily need props for dramatizations!) Choose volunteers and repeat the song three times, one time for each spider. Give your cloud actor confetti, or a water sprayer for his part. Remind your spider actors to portray their size. For example, the GREAT BIG SPIDER will take GREAT BIG STEPS! Also, try giving the part of the largest spider to your smallest student and vice versa and see what happens? After the children know the song well, another way to enhance the dramatization is by using classroom instruments for sound effects. See the following page for suggestions. Try using a large drum and cymbals for the GREAT BIG SPIDER. What will you find for the teeny weeny spider? Be creative!

Related Literature:

Eency Weency Spider, by Joanne Oppenheim
I Love Spiders, by Rita Parkinson
Spiders and Webs, by Carolyn Lunn
Spider's Web, by Christine Back and Barrie Watts
The Very Busy Spider, by Eric Carle

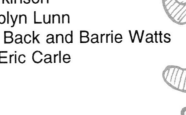

EENCY WEENCY SPIDER SOUND EFFECTS
By Silvia León

Cymbals
Sound of the spider when it is washed away

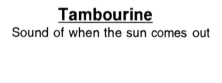

Tambourine
Sound of when the sun comes out

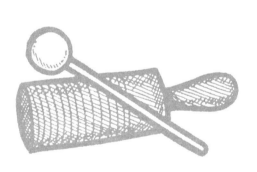

Tone Block
Sound of the spider going up the water spout

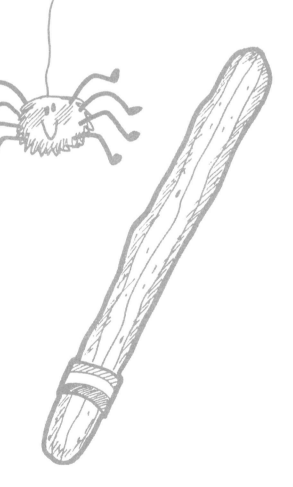

Rainstick
Sound of the rain coming down

49

DANCING SPIDERS ON A WEB

By Silvia León

Materials Needed:

- a spider book
- a very long piece of cord, roving, or rope
- spider music
- objects (furniture or playground equipment)
- chart paper

Procedure:

1) Read to your children a book on how spiders build their webs, such as The Very Busy Spider, by Eric Carle. Point out how spiders attach the string of their webs to objects so that the wind won't blow it away.

2) Ask your children how they would build a spider web if they were very tiny spiders. How about if they were VERY BIG SPIDERS? Brainstorm creative answers. Chart them down.

3) Next, have your children pretend to be spiders spinning a web. Give a cord to a child and let him choose a beginning place for a spider web. Then give to another and another child until everyone has had a chance to attach their web to an object. Encourage creative places.

4) When the web is done, play some type of spider music (Artsplay, by Leon Burton and Kathy Kuroda or Spin, Spider, Spin by Marsha Bergman). Have three children at one time dance over, under, through and around the web's cords. Encourage children to twist, bend, swing, tip-toe, etc. The entire class should not be spiders all at one time because children may get very excited, and since there will be many cords tied all over the place, this may create a hazardous condition. Three or four at a time is perfect!

TWINKLE, TWINKLE LITTLE STAR
Traditional

C
Twinkle, twinkle little star,
       F C

F   C   G₇   C
How I wonder what you are.

     F   C   G₇
Up above the world so high

C   F   C   G₇
like a diamond in the sky.

C   F C
Twinkle, twinkle little star,

F   C   G₇   C
How I wonder what you are.

A Variation!
By Silvia Leon

Pretty, pretty little star

In the ocean very far.

Leave the water and come near

So that we can play right here.

Pretty, pretty, little star,

In the ocean very far.

BRILLA, BRILLA ESTRELLITA

Translation by Silvia León

    C   F   C
Brilla , brilla estrellita,
F   C   G₇   C
Como pienso adonde estas.
       F   C   G₇
Lejos del mundo grande
C   F   C   G₇
Brillas como un diamante.
    C   F   C
Brilla, brilla estrellita,
F   C   G₇   C
Como pienso adonde estas.

¡Una Variación!
por Silvia León

Linda, linda estrellita

En el mar tan bonita.

Deja el mar y ven aca

¡A jugar conmigo ya!

Linda, linda estrellita

En el mar tan bonita.

TWINKLE, TWINKLE LITTLE STAR
Lesson Plan
(By Silvia Leon)

Age Group
3 - 6 year olds

Materials Needed
Twinkle, Twinkle Little Star felt figures, objects that twinkle (such as a diamond ring, sequins, rhine stones, etc.), a tray with an assortment of objects of various shapes (include a sheriff's badge, a starfish, and other star-shaped objects), two stars of identical sizes, glow-in-the-dark stars for each of your students (see the pattern on page 56).

Objectives
After singing and discussing Twinkle, Twinkle Little Star several times, the children will:

- memorize the song
- share feelings about the darkness
- identify star-shaped objects
- discuss the meaning of twinkle
- learn that the sun is also a star
- be introduced to Earth as the planet we live on

Note:
You may want to do this lesson in 2 or 3 parts, depending on your student's age and attention span.

Procedure:
1. Place the felt star with a face on it on you flannel board. Tell your students that today you will teach them a song about a little star in the night sky. Sing the song completely. Now sing a phrase and let the children repeat what you have sung. Do this all the way through the song.

2. Show the children that a star has 5 pointy arms. Count them together. Show them how our hands also look like stars if we spread our fingers out wide. We have five pointy fingers too! Count together. Who can show me their hand star?

3. Now sing the song again using hand motions. Lift your hand way up high with fingers spread outward. This will be your star. Move wrist back and forth for twinkling. Put arms together above head like a big ball for "up above the world so high".

4. Ask the children what they think twinkle means. Accept all answers. Show them a tray of sparkling (twinkling) objects, such as sequins, glitter, rhinestones, a diamond ring, etc. Pass the objects around. Twinkle means that it sparkles and shines like the objects on the tray.

5. Present another tray with objects of various shapes. Pick volunteers to pick out the star-shaped objects.

* This is a good place to stop. You may want to follow-up with an activity such as making star-shaped sandwiches or do star sponge painting.

6. Place the felt stars on your flannel board. Ask your students if anyone has ever seen a real star. Where? Was it daytime or nighttime? What else can be seen in the sky at night? Brainstorm for creative answers (airplanes, fireworks, spaceships, etc.).

7. Place the moon, sun, and clouds on your flannel board. Which of these things can we see in the sky at night and which can we see during the day? Can clouds be seen at night as well as during the day? Why can't we see the sun at night?

8. Place the Earth felt piece on the flannel board. Tell the children that Earth is the planet we live on. The Earth twirls 'round and 'round. When we face the sun it is daytime and when we don't face the sun it is nighttime. (This is a difficult

concept for young children to understand. You may want to further illustrate with a globe and a bright light or flashlight). At night we cannot see the sun because it is on the other side of the Earth. Did you know that the sun is really a star that is very close to the Earth? All stars give light just like the sun, but because they are so far away from us they look very little.

9. Ask the children if anyone likes the nighttime. Why or why not? Is anyone afraid of the dark? Let the children share their feelings openly. Tell them that it's okay to be afraid of the darkness. Many people feel this way too. Talk about things they can do to not be so afraid (hug a teddy bear, keep a night light on, sleep with mommy, etc.). What do people use to see at night? Did you know that in some places out in the country people put fireflies in a jar and use them as lanterns?

10) **Grand Finale!** Give each child a glow-in-the-dark star puppet (see page 56). Make sure that when you turn your lights off, your classroom is pitch dark. If not, go to a bathroom or any other room where <u>no</u> light will come in. Place immature children who may be frightened by the darkness next to an adult. Turn off the lights and oooo!! ahhhh!! The stars glow!! Sing Twinkle, Twinkle Little Star again, moving the star stick puppets from side to side. Your students will love it! Grown-ups too!

Related Literature:

Como Son Las Estrellas, by Roy Wandelmaier (available in English)
Draw Me A Star, by Eric Carle
Fireflies in the Night, by Judy Hawes
Goodnight, Goodnight, by Eve Rice
Happy Birthday Moon, by Frank Asch
La Luna, El Sol y Las Estrellas, by John Lewellen (available in English)
The Nappy House, by Audrey and Don Wood
Night in the Country, by Cynthia Rylant
The Tiny Star, by Arthur Ginolfi
Twinkle, Twinkle, a Golden Sound Story, by Tim O'Brien

GLOW-IN-THE-DARK STAR

by Silvia León

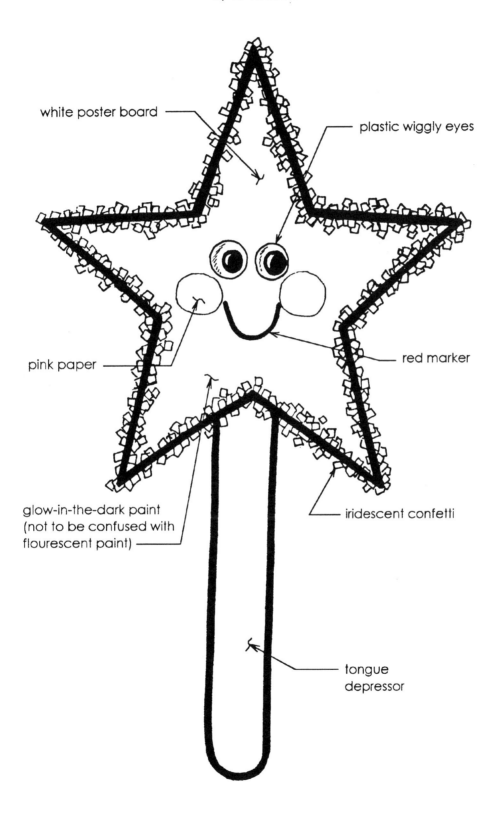

white poster board

plastic wiggly eyes

pink paper

glow-in-the-dark paint
(not to be confused with
flourescent paint)

red marker

iridescent confetti

tongue
depressor

Twinkle, Twinkle, Little Star Song Chart for Hand Bells

by Silvia León

(White Butcher Paper 7 ft. x 2 ft.)

red · turquoise · turquoise · blue · blue · turquoise · green · green · yellow · yellow · orange · orange · red

turquoise · turquoise · green · yellow · yellow · orange · turquoise · turquoise · green · green · yellow · yellow · orange

red · turquoise · turquoise · blue · blue · turquoise · green · green · yellow · yellow · orange · orange · red

Cut ovals from color paper and glue onto the white butcher paper. (color xeroxing paper works best since construction paper will fade.)

The color of the ovals correspond with the color of the hand bells.
This hand bell chart is to be used with Accurate Tone FMT Hand Bells.

Hand bells may be purchased from any major educational catalog.

STARRY, STARRY NIGHT PAINTING

By Silvia León

Materials Needed:

- large pieces of construction paper in dark colors (dark blue, black, or purple)
- glow-in-the-dark paint in a variety of colors
- small star sequins in a variety of colors
- paintbrushes
- paint aprons
- song: Starry, Starry Night, by Don McLean
- Poster of Vincent van Gogh's painting, Starry Night

Procedure:

1) Show children the painting Starry Night by Vincent Van Gogh.

2) Talk about the swirl shapes he painted that give movement to the painting.

3) Discuss the dark and light colors he used to give a starry night effect.

4) Tell the children that when an artist makes a painting, sometimes it may look like something and sometimes not. An artist paints what he sees or what he feels or what he imagines inside his mind. Ask your students if they think Vincent Van Gogh painted what he saw, felt, or imagined (all three). This is what makes Starry Night so beautiful and special! It is unique and different, like no one else's.

5) Ask the children to make their own Starry Night painting, like no one else's. Tell them they can paint something they see, feel, or imagine.

> Have children choose a dark colored piece of construction paper.
> Tell your students that they can paint a starry anything! For example, a starry cat, a starry sun, a starry feeling, or just starry colors!
> While children paint their starry masterpieces, play the song Starry, Starry Night by Don McLean next to the painting easels.
> When the paintings dry, have the children glue star sequins wherever they want.
> Let the children choose a title starting with "Starry, Starry . . . "
> When the paintings are hung on display, they twinkle when the lights are on, but when the lights are off . . . OOOOOO!! Magnificent!! They glow!

WHERE IS THUMBKIN ?

Traditional

C
Where is Thumbkin?

Where is Thumbkin?

Here I am. Here I am.

How are you today sir?

Very well and thank you.

Run away. Run away.

Where is Pointer...
Where is Tall Man...
Where is Ring Man...
Where is Pinky...

Where's the family?
Where's the family?
Here we are. Here we are.
Here we are together,
We'll play with you forever.
Run away. Run away.

59

PULGARCITO

Translation by Silvia León

C

Pulgarcito,

Pulgarcito,

¿Dónde estás? ¿Dónde estás?

Aquí estoy amigo.

Juega aquí conmigo.

Ya me voy. Ya me voy.

*La que apunta...
Señor Alto...
Anillito...
Chiquitito...

La familia,
La familia,
¿Dónde están? ¿Dónde están?
Aquí estamos amigo.
Jugando aquí contigo.
Vamonos. Vamonos.

*In Spanish, fingers are masculine. Therefore, use "La que apunta" only when using the female felt finger puppet designed to accompany this song. Otherwise, use "Apuntito" as the name for the index finger.

WHERE IS THUMBKIN ?
Lesson Plan
By Silvia León

Age Group:
3 - 6 year olds

Materials Needed:
Where is Thumbkin felt finger puppets, a brown paper bag for each student with 5 different objects inside, chart paper and finger puppets for each student (This is optional but will really help children learn which finger to show while singing the song). You will need 2 finger puppets in blue, red, green, yellow and pink for every child. Ask parents or a nearby business to donate knitted gloves in these colors. Cut off the fingers and paint eyes and mouths with fabric paint. **Thumbkins** are blue, **Pointers** are red, **Tall Mans** are green, **Ring Mans** are yellow and **Pinkys** are pink.

Objectives:
After singing the song, <u>Where is Thumbkin?</u> several times and discussing concepts related to it, the child will:

- match fingers to finger names in the song
- coordinate finger movements
- learn different parts of the hand (palm, fingers, nails)
- compare and contrast different sizes, skin color and textures of hands
- learn the many functions of hands
- identify objects in a bag using the sense of touch

Procedure:
1. Have your students look at their hands. What does the top look like? (fingers, fingernails, hair) What does the bottom look like? (wrinkles and lines) Tell your students this part of the hand is called the palm.

2. Have your children put their hands on the floor or table and compare the many different sizes and skin tones. Discuss that some hands can be young, others old and some even hairy!

61

3. How many things can your hands do? Brainstorm answers and chart them down. Now read the chart and do what the children suggested (clapping, waving, scratching, wiggling, waving, drawing, playing the piano, etc.)

4. Tell your students that today they will learn a new song called Where is Thumbkin?

   - Show your students your thumb and tell them this short and chubby finger is called the thumb. Now put your Thumbkin puppet on and pass out the blue finger puppets to your students. Sing the first verse and have the children repeat after you.
   - Next introduce Pointer. She is red and likes to point at things. Practice pointing at things with your students. Now pass out the red finger puppets and sing this verse.
   - Have your children look at their hands and find the tallest finger. Put your green finger puppets on and tell them that this one is called Tall Man. Sing this verse.
   - The next finger is called Ring Man because on this finger people usually wear rings. Put the yellow finger puppets on. This will be the most difficult finger for your children to lift while holding down the rest!
   - Have your children look at their hands again and find the smallest finger. Tell them that this one is Pinky and she has a baby voice.   Put on your pink finger puppets and sing this verse using a high pitched voice.
   - Finally, bring out all the fingers for the last verse and sing in a low and loud voice!

5. **Grand Finale!** Give each student a brown paper bag with approximately 5 objects inside. Each bag should have the same items. Without peeking, ask your children to take out an object. How does your hand know? Does it have eyes? (Here is a perfect opportunity to do a follow-up lesson on how blind and deaf people use their hands to feel things and to communicate.)

Related Literature:
Where is Thumbkin? by Pam Schiller and Thomas Moore
Hand, Hand, Fingers, Thumb by Al Perkins
Piggies by Don and Audrey Wood
The Handmade Alphabet by Laura Rankin

PEANUT BUTTER & JELLY "HANDWICH"

By Silvia León

Materials Needed:

- peanut butter (Buy the creamy kind that spreads smoothly so the bread doesn't tear!)
- jelly
- small cups for the peanut butter and jelly
- bread
- plastic knives
- paper plates
- hand-shaped cookie cutters
- milk

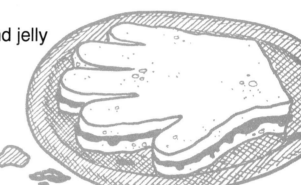

Procedure:

1. If you are going to be working with four children, then prepare 4 small cups with peanut butter and 4 with jelly so each child have their own. You will also need 4 hand cookie cutters as well. In fact, 4 of everything! (This will avoid many headaches, prevent grabbing and jars tipping and keep the peace among impatient little hands.)

2. Demonstrate how to make a peanut butter and jelly sandwich. (Remember to wash your hands and insist that your children wash them too.)

3. Now pass out a paper plate to each child, 2 slices of bread, a plastic knife and the small cups containing the peanut butter and jelly.

4. Let them spread their own peanut butter on one slice of bread and jelly on the other.

5. After they put both slices together, demonstrate how to use the hand shape cookie cutter. Now let them do it. Not only have they made a " handwich" but if they carefully removed it, they'll see the empty hand shape left in the bread…a positive and negative design!

6. Eat right away with a glass of milk or save in a plastic sandwich bag until snack time! Don't forget to write the children's names on the baggies!

SHAVING CREAM FINGERPAINTING
By Silvia León

Materials Needed:
shaving cream (You'll need about 1 can per 10 children)
food color (an assortment of different colors)
plastic aprons
a smooth table
white art paper

Procedure:
Give your children many opportunities to play with shaving cream. The tactile experience is wonderful. Encourage the children to use their fingertips to make lines, swirls, shapes and for those who are ready, letters and numbers. Let them explore squishing the lather between their fingers and splattering it with their palms.

The nice thing about shaving cream is that it is completely washable. Outdoor tables are preferable for the freedom they offer children (they don't have to worry about getting the floors messy) and it's also a great way to get the tables washed! Don't clean the tables in between groups. Just put more shaving cream right on top because whatever is left behind tends to evaporate and smooth out. With a nearby hose, squirt off the table top when the last child is through.

Have your children wear plastic aprons. Plain shaving cream washes right off hands, hair and clothes, but if you use food coloring, unprotected clothes will get stained.

Once your students have had opportunities to play with shaving cream, add a new dimension by introducing colors to it. Squirt out shaving cream on a smooth table and let the children start playing in it. Then add drops from 3 different food colors. Let them mix it.

Before your children turn the colors into mud place a sheet of white art paper over the colored shaving cream for a beautiful pastel swirl of colors. Then add more shaving cream and drops of food coloring for the children to continue exploring and creating whatever they want.

MISTER SUN

Traditional (additional verses by Silvia León)

Oh Mister Sun, sun (D)

Mister Golden Sun, (E7)

Please shine down on me. (A7) (D)

Oh Mister Sun, sun (D)

Mister Golden Sun, (E7)

Hiding behind a tree. (A7)

These little children are asking you (D) (A7)

To please come out so we can play with you. (D) (A7)

(repeat first verse)

Oh Mister Cloud, cloud, Mister Chubby Cloud,
Please rain down on me...
Oh Mister Wind, wind, Mister Breezy Wind
Please blow down on me...
Oh Misses Snow, snow, Misses Freezing Snow
Please fall down on me...
Oh Misses Rainbow, rainbow, Misses Pretty Rainbow
Paint the sky for me...

SEÑOR SOL

Translation by Silvia León

D
O Señor Sol, sol

E7
Dorado Señor Sol,

A7   D
Brilla para mí.

D
O Señor Sol, sol

E7
Dorado Señor Sol,

A7
Detraz del árbol allí.

D   A7
Estos niños te suplican a tí

D   A7
Que por favor ven a jugar aquí.

(repitan el primer verso)

O Señor Nube, nube, gordito Señor Nube,
Llueve para mí...
O Señor Viento, viento, suave Señor Viento
Sopla para mí...
Señora Nieve, nieve, copito de nieve,
Cae arriba de mí...
Señora Iris, Iris, linda arco iris
Pinta el cielo para mí...

MISTER SUN
Lesson Plan
By Silvia León

Age Group:
3-6 year olds

Materials Needed:
Mister Sun flannel board felt characters, a flannel board, tambourines, a rainstick, an autoharp, jingle bells, an umbrella for each child, a hose with a spray nozzle.

Objectives:
After singing Mr. Sun several times and discussing parts of the song the children will:

- learn new words related to weather
- creatively express weather elements through movement
- make weather sounds with musical instruments
- talk about and experience weather play activities

Procedure:
1. Go outside your classroom and look up at the sky. Ask the children what they see. Tell them that everyday things in the sky change. Sometimes there are a few clouds, sometimes many. The sun shines on some days and on other days there is rain or snow. Sometimes, if we're lucky, we may even see a rainbow. At times, it can be cold outside, warm or hot. All these things make up the weather.

2. Return to your classroom. Tell your children that today you will teach them a song about the weather called Mister Sun.

3. Place all the felt weather characters on the flannel board. Point to the sun and tell them that his name is Mister Sun. Ask your children what they think the other character's names are.

67

4. Sing the Mister Sun verse and have the children repeat after you. Now try singing the other verses with your students.

5. Add sound effects. After "Please shine down on me," stop and have a couple of children shake a tambourine. After, "Please rain down on me," have a couple of children turn over a rainstick. After, "Please blow down on me," everybody takes a deep breathe and blows out air. After "Please fall down on me" a few children can ring jingle bells. After, "Paint the sky for me," have a child hold down any autoharp key and slowly strum upward.

6. Add hand motions. Let the children help you. Ask them how they can show with their body that the sun is shining or that the wind is blowing, etc. This is a great song to incorporate sign language, if you know any!

7. Discuss the words in the song. How would you play in the sun? ...in the rain? ...in the wind? ...in the snow? ...with a rainbow?

8. **Grand Finale!** This can be a follow-up lesson...an Umbrella Day! (Bring a couple of your own umbrellas for those children who forget to bring one.) Now go for an umbrella walk around the school. This is a perfect activity if you're lucky enough to have a rainy day. If not, climb up on your playground apparatus with a hose and tell the kids that you are a big, gray cloud and to prepare themselves under their umbrellas for a storm. Squirt them first with a gentle mist and progress to a downpour! If you're brave enough, let your students take turns being the gray cloud and you get under an umbrella together with the rest of your class! Warning! This activity is too much fun and everyone, including yourself, will probably laugh and scream. Therefore, it is definitely recommended only for the young at heart!!!

Related Literature:
Billy Bean, by Maria Elena Buria
Dreams, by Peter Spier
It looked Like Spilt Milk, by Charles G. Shaw
The Snowy day, by Ezra Jack Keats
The Umbrella Day, by Nancy Evans Cooney

HOW TO MAKE A RAINSTICK

By Silvia León

Materials Needed:

- a very sturdy cardboard tube at least 2 ft. long from clothing factories or blueprint shops
- flat head nails slightly shorter in length than the diameter of your cardboard tube (You will need ALOT of nails so buy a large box!)
- two round pieces of cardboard to glue to the ends of the tube
- book binding or electrical tape
- hot glue gun & hot glue
- rice, crushed seashells or small pebbles

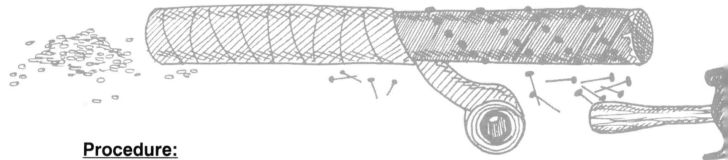

Procedure:

1. Hammer nails into the cardboard tube. Start at one end and spiral downward.
2. Hot glue one of the round cardboard pieces to only one end of the tube.
3. Experiment time! Hold your cardboard tube upright and add about half a cup of rice, crushed shells or small pebbles through the open end. If it goes straight through to the bottom, then you need to hammer more nails to your tube. If the rice (or whatever other object you're using inside) becomes blocked at different levels, you have too many nails. Play around, adding or subtracting nails until your rice, seashells or small pebbles sound like rain as it trickles down through the tube.
4. When you have just the right sound, hot glue the other piece of cardboard to the top.
5. Use electrical tape or book binding tape to completely cover the tube. This will not only keep the nails from falling out, but it will make your rainstick more attractive and safer to use.
6. Enjoy your homemade rainstick!

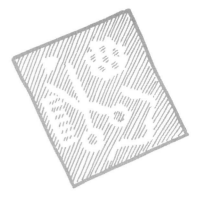

SUN - SATIONAL PRINTS

By Silvia León

Materials Needed:

- Large sheets of dark colored construction paper (black, purple, red, dark green or blue)
- a variety of interesting objects, preferably flat (rope, scissors, lace, paper clips, leaves, flowers, a fork, geometric shapes, etc.)
- masking tape

Procedure:

1. Ask your classroom children to look for 10 or more objects either from home or from the classroom that have interesting shapes. Give them a couple of examples.

2. Let them select among a variety of dark colored construction paper.

3. Tape the children's construction paper on a table or floor that has direct, full sunlight all day long. Make a sign warning other classrooms not to touch.

4. Let your children arrange the objects they selected in any way onto their construction paper. Lightweight objects such as feathers or leaves will need to be taped to the paper or they may blow away. Roll a piece of tape to the back of the item to keep it stationary. This activity is NOT recommended on a windy day!

5. Leave the objects on the construction paper for the entire day. Come back in the afternoon, take the objects off the paper and...VOILA! You and your children will discover "sun-sational" art prints!

There are also commercial, sun-sensitive papers you can purchase from educational stores and catalogs. The price for 30 students costs about $15.00. You will find this type of paper under the name of Sunlight Magic Kits.

HEAD AND SHOULDERS
Traditional

A
Head and shoulders,
Knees and toes, knees and toes.

Head and shoulders,
E
Knees and toes, knees and toes.

A   D
Eyes and ears and mouth and nose.

E
Head and shoulders,
A
Knees and toes, knees and toes.

Arms and legs,
Bellybutton, bellybutton.

Arms and legs,
Bellybutton, bellybutton.

Hair and eyebrows, cheeks and chin.

Arms and legs,
Bellybutton, bellybutton.

71

CABEZA Y HOMBROS

Translation by Silvia León

A
Cabeza y hombros,
Rodillas y pies, rodillas y pies.

Cabeza y hombros,
E
Rodillas y pies, rodillas y pies.

A   D
Ojos y orejas, boca y nariz.

E
Cabeza y hombros,
A
Rodillas y pies, rodillas y pies.

Brazos, piernas,
Ombligo, ombligo.

Brazos, piernas,
Ombligo, ombligo.

Pelo y cejas, mejillas, barbilla.

Brazos, piernas,
Ombligo, ombligo.

HEAD AND SHOULDERS
Lesson Plan
By Silvia León

Age Group:

3 - 6 year olds

Materials Needed:

Head and Shoulders flannel board felt figures, a large flannel board, a red, a yellow and a blue hula hoop, the book <u>Your Bellybutton</u>, by Jun Nanao.

Objectives:

After discussing body and facial parts using the felt figures and singing the song Head and Shoulders, the children will:

- be able to name the main parts of a face
- know the function of the eyes, nose, mouth and ears
- identify from memory missing facial parts
- correctly place facial parts onto a blank felt face
- be more aware of different types of skin tones, hair and eyes
- be able to name at least 5 body parts
- know the function of certain body parts
- be able to correctly arrange arms, legs, head and torso to complete a felt body on the flannel board
- rearrange from memory scrambled body parts

Special Note to Teachers:

The following plans, although very simple, should be divided into several days because in-depth discussions and feelings may surface when talking about differences in people. Use your own judgment and let the children's attention span guide you as to how much or how little you will present on any given day. You will find suggested places to stop in the lesson plan.

Procedure:

1. Tell your children that today they will be learning about parts of the face. You can quickly assess who knows their facial parts by telling them to touch their nose, eyes, ears, cheeks, eyebrows, etc. Those children who aren't sure will look around to copy their neighbors or point incorrectly.

2. Begin by talking about skin. Explain to your students that skin is like a coat that covers the entire face and body. Ask them what they think would happen if people didn't have any skin. Skin, like hair and eyes come in different colors. Some people have darker and some lighter skin tones. Have the children put out their hands straight forward, palms downward, and compare the different shades of skin among their classmates.

3. This is a good opportunity to talk about different races and ethnic groups. Your children may have many feelings, misconceptions, attitudes and prejudices, even at this early age, that you may want to discuss in depth with them. Follow the interest and needs of your classroom children.

4. Now ask your students to stand up. Tell them you are going to sing a new song today called Head and Shoulders. Sing a phrase and have them repeat after you. Now sing the song together again, touching the body parts mentioned in the song. Sing it faster, then faster, then super fast. The children love this because it's almost impossible to touch all the body parts when you're singing really fast and everyone gets confused...including yourself!

(This is a good ending point. You may want to continue with the rest of the lesson plan on another day.)

5. Sing the song, Head and Shoulders again. Now place the blank felt face on the flannel board. Ask your students what parts are missing from the face. Give volunteers different facial pieces and let them arrange the face. Evaluate together. Does the face look right? Are the eyebrows in the correct place?

6. After the face is put together correctly tell the children you're going to play a game. Have them look closely at the face. Then tell them to close their eyes and ... no peeking. Now remove a facial part (the nose, for example) and then tell the children to open their eyes and guess what's missing. Continue this game until the face is blank again. You may also ask them what's different? For

example, instead of removing the eyes, change them for another set of felt eyes in a different color.

7. Ask the children how many things they can think of that they can do with their eyes (for example, blink, cry, stare, wink, sleep, see, etc.). What can you do with your mouth? ...your nose? ...your ears? ...your cheeks? ...your eyelashes? Etc.

(Here is another place where you might want to stop and continue on another day.)

8. Sing the song <u>Head and Shoulders</u> again. Review parts of the face from yesterday. Then tell your children that today they will be learning about parts of the body.

9. Ask your children to point to certain parts of their body. Again, by observing their responses, you will be able to easily assess who knows their body parts and who doesn't .

10. Now bring out the flannel board pieces. Place the torso of the little boy on the flannel board and then give the head, arms and legs to volunteers so that together they assemble him. Discuss all the different parts.

11. Place the torso of the little girl on the flannel board and again give the rest of the body pieces to other children so with everyone's help she is assembled. Again review the different body parts. How is the boy the same as the girl? How are they different?

12. Ask a boy and a girl volunteer to come up and compare how they are alike and different. Now ask everyone to stand up. Who is the tallest, shortest, has the longest hair, etc.?

13. Use different color hula hoops to sort your classroom children (for example, everyone wearing a dress stands inside the yellow hoop, everyone with curly hair in the blue hoop and everyone wearing pants in the red hoop). Let the children make up the rules for the sets.

(Here again is another place to stop and continue on the following day.)

14. Review the body parts from the previous day. Ask the children to sit down and tell them they need to close their eyes for a game you're going to play with them. Now rearrange the body parts so nothing is where it should be (for example, the girl's head is on the boy's neck, the feet are where the arms should be, etc.) Tell your students to open their eyes. Ask them, "What's wrong with these bodies?" Let volunteers come up to fix them.

15. Discuss the various functions of different body parts. What can you do with your legs? ...your neck? ...your hands? ...your shoulders? ...your feet? ...your knees? ...your waist? ...your elbows? Etc.

16. Now point to the navel (bellybutton) on either the girl or boy felt figure and ask the children if they know what this is called. What is it used for? Does everybody have one? Why?

17. **Grande Finale!** Read the book, <u>Your Bellybutton</u> by Jun Nanao. This is the story of a little boy who doesn't like his bellybutton because it sticks out. The colorful, child-like story explains in simple terms how the bellybutton is an important mark of your birth from your mother and how your body was connected to her body by a cord that was attached to your bellybutton.

Related Literature:
<u>A Kaleidoscope of Kids,</u> by Emma Damon
<u>Everyone Poops,</u> by Taro Gomi
<u>Faces,</u> by Shelly Rotner and Ken Kreisler
<u>Famous Faces,</u> by Norman Messenger
<u>Look Inside Your Body,</u> by Gina Ingoglia
<u>Make a Face</u>, by Henry and Amy Schwartz
<u>Outside-in,</u> by Clare Smallman
<u>The Holes in Your Nose,</u> by Genichiro Yagyu
<u>Your Bellybutton,</u> by Jun Nanao

Copy, cut out and laminate the name strips below. By adding a small dot of velcro or sandpaper on the back they can now be used on the flannel board to name the various body parts in English and/or Spanish.

head	cuello
shoulders	hombros
knees	rodillas
toes	dedos
eyes	ojos
ears	orejas
mouth	boca
nose	nariz

hands	manos
feet	pies
arms	brazos
legs	piernas
bellybutton	ombligo
hair	pelo
eyebrows	cejas
cheeks	mejillas
chin	barbilla

PAINTING CHEEK-TO-CHEEK

By Silvia León

Materials Needed:

- face make-up sticks (hypo-allergenic type)
- face tissue and wet wipes
- individual mirrors (the kind that stand up on their own)
- painting smocks
- the book Face Painting, by the editors of Klutz Press

Procedure:

1. Cover a table with a plastic tablecloth. Provide a painting smock, a box of face make-up sticks and a self-standing mirror for each child at the table. Also, a box of facial tissue and wet wipes should be available in case they want to wipe off something from their face that they dislike.

2. Begin by talking about face painting. Who wears paint on their face? (Clowns, mostly women but some men do wear make-up too, actresses and actors, people from various cultures.) Show them magazine pictures of people wearing make-up or books such as Face Painting, by Klutz Press.

3. To show children the technique, demonstrate on your own face. (Cheeks and foreheads are great for drawing simple designs. Don't forget your nose and chin. How about earrings?) Your students will love watching you do this!

4. I do not recommend using whiteface because it is very messy and young kids tend to get it in their hair, eyes, nose and even ears! This technique is best for an adult to apply on children. However, I prefer just the stick make-up when children are working independently.

5. The important thing is that YOU or other adults do not paint any child's face. Yes, the children will have beautiful designs done by adults but...this will not be a learning experience for the children. Remember that the learning and the fun is in the process!

6. Have faith in your students and let them independently paint their own face. Kid-to-kid face painting is also fun. Allow them to keep their face on to show their parents and friends when they go home. Keep yours on as well!

DOUBLE-SIDED "ME"

By Silvia León

Materials Needed:

- white butcher paper (cut into 4ft. strips)
- skin tone and tempera paint in all colors
- thick markers in all colors
- buttons, zippers, lace and yarn in a variety of hair color
- painting smocks

Procedure:

1. Have the children lay on a piece of white butcher paper on the floor. An adult (parents are great for this job!) will trace around the body with a pencil. Encourage the children to lay in creative poses. However, they must lay flat on their backs. (The adults who draw around the children's bodies must keep their pencils completely perpendicular and not inclined, otherwise the body will come out too skinny and distorted.)

2. Once the bodies are drawn, adults should make the clothing boarders. (For example, draw a line across the neck where the blouse or shirt begins, the sleeves, the pants, etc.)

3. Now the fun begins! Put painting smocks on your children and have them paint all the skin areas first and then their clothes. Wait a day for the paint to dry. Do not put facial features yet. (Have adults cut out the painted body, trace onto another piece of white butcher paper, cut out and staple together leaving an opening to stuff with newspapers later on.)

4. Now the children will paint the back side of their bodies in the same colors they used for the front. Wait another day for it to dry.

5. The children may now add facial features and clothing patterns with markers. Next, they can glue the yarn for hair and buttons, zippers and lace for added touches in their clothing. (Adults can help make braids and pigtails for hair.)

6. Have an adult stuff the figures with newspapers and staple shut. Now you have 3-D self-portraits of your classroom children. Pose them throughout your room for your "Back to School Night". (Here are some suggestions: Pose children playing house, on a rocking chair, playing next to the sand table, painting, etc. Add name tag necklaces. Finally, use tape and fish string to help you pose the figures. Parents and kids will love this!)

NEW TEACHER SUGGESTED ACTIVITIES

How to make simple finger puppets and stick puppets:
Save the white scraps of felt, cut them into 1/4" wide strips, form into rings for fingers and seal using fabric glue or a hot glue gun. Attach a small dot of the hook side of Velcro to each ring. Now they are ready to be used with the felt characters as finger puppets. A dot of the hook side of Velcro can be placed on a tongue depressor or popsicle stick to make stick puppets.

- Mr. Sun can be coordinated with the rain cycle for a full unit on the weather as well as appropriate clothing for each type of weather.

- Use the tree from the Monkeys in the Tree with Mr. Sun to hide charters behind. Use the moon from Twinkle Star to add a verse about Mr. Moon. ("Mr. Moon, moon, Bright and Shinny Moon, Please shine down on me.")

- Head and Shoulders is a wonderful vehicle for exploring and naming body parts and how each functions. Here is a wonderful comparison of how we are all similar, although we have many differences, i.e. skin color, hair and eye color, size, etc.

- Thumbkin can be used to show how each of us has a unique finger and foot print. Using washable ink pads, have the children make thumb prints on a piece of white paper. Add features to make faces and animals. Here is a fun, creative art project!

- Give 10 students a felt number from the 10 Children. Be sure they know what number they have. Now direct the children to move into place by number. For example: "#1 stand in the front of the room and face the class, #2 stand behind #1, #3 stand in front of #1, #4 stand next to #2, #5 hold your number below #3, etc. When you are done review positions and place value 1st, 2nd, 3rd,...last. This activity is excellent for learning to follow directions as well as a review of directionality, laterality and ordinal numbers

- Given the various races and challenges depicted in the Ten Children, think of all the social studies units that could be taught. Does being different in various ways effect the way we work or play individually or together?

- After Halloween, the pumpkin set could be used to do a unit on emotions and feelings associated with various facial expressions

- The pumpkins can also be incorporated into units on fruits, vegetables, nutrition or plant growth, as well as the farm unit.

- Compare the chicks and ducks to show how living things grow and develop differently. Both are hatched from eggs and start out as little yellow, fuzzy two footed birds of about the same size. They certainly grow up to be quite different. (And don't we all?) Discuss the specific differences with the children. This discussion could be expanded to include plants and animals. A wonderful place to read the Ugly Duckling story to illustrate these differences.

- Begin a study of science and nature using <u>5 Little Speckled Frogs.</u> Include the study of frogs, insects and the pond environment.

- The <u>Eency Weency Spider</u> might be extended into a unit on spiders: i.e. how many legs does a spider have? (8) How many eyes do they have? (8) What kind of animal is a spider? (arachnids)   A unit on rain and the rain cycle would be appropriate at this time. Be sure to discuss and show the "waterspout".

- Make edible spiders using 2 vanilla wafers for the body, chow mein noodles for the legs, raisins for the eyes. Use peanut butter to glue the vanilla wafers together. Be sure to place the legs inside (4 on each side) before sealing the wafers. peanut butter will hold the raisins in place. Add red licorice mouths if desired.

- Compare the <u>Monkeys on the Bed</u> and the <u>5 Little Speckled Frogs</u> or <u>Monkeys in the Tree</u> to explain the difference between fact and fantasy. Although, <u>Monkeys on the Bed</u> are adorable and lots of fun, the children should be asked if monkeys really wear pajamas, do they sleep on this kind of a bed, does Mama really call the Doctor? They are just fun and fantasy. However, frogs do sit on logs, do jump into the pond and do eat insects, and monkeys do sit in trees and might be eaten by crocodiles.

- The words to <u>Monkeys on the Bed</u> can be sung to the melody of <u>Short'nin'</u> <u>Bread</u>, a plantation song. (This works only in the English version.)

- Use the pajamas the <u>Monkeys on the Bed</u> are wearing to review colors.

- <u>Monkeys in a Tree</u> could be used to show directionality and laterality. Using the numbered monkeys direct the children to move them above, below, next to, in, outside, beside, etc., the tree. Start with one direction and build to a series of two, three or more commands given at a time.

- The frogs, chicks, ducks, spiders, pumpkins, and <u>Mr. Sun</u> sets could be incorporated into the farm unit.

- Use both sets of monkeys, the frogs, spider, and weather (<u>Mr. Sun</u>) to begin a unit on the rain forest.

- Use <u>Twinkle Star</u> for lessons on the basics of the universe. Where does the sun go when it sets? Why can't we see the stars during the day? Can people visit the moon? Talk about the sun as being a star that is very close to the earth. Earth is a planet. Are there other plants, and can we see them? When we see them, what do planets look like? (They look like stars.) Here is a great beginning for the space unit.

- Change the words to the first two lines and last two lines of <u>Twinkle Star</u> as follows:
  Twinkle, twinkle, little   <u>(name)</u> , *(name and point to a child, who stands)*
  How we love just who you are! *(hands are placed over heart.}*
  On second twinkle, twinkle , little <u>(name)</u> , *(point to child, who takes a bow.)*
  How we love just who you are! *(hands are placed over heart; child sits down.}*

ADDITIONAL RELATED LITERATURE

Little Green Frog, by Rozanne Williams
Miss Fanny Frog, by Frog Street Press
Our Pumpkin, by Rozanne Williams
Nuestra Calabaza, by Rozanne Williams
It's a Fruit, It's a Vegetable, It's a Pumpkin, by Allan Fowler
The Chick and the Duckling, by Mirra Ginsburg
Pollito y Patito, by Mirra Ginsburg
A Rainbow of Friends, by P.K. Hallinan
Spiders Are Not Insects, by Allan Fowler
The Great Thumbprint Book, by Ed Emberly
The Ugly Duckling, Various Versions are available

RESOURCE MATERIALS

Alphabet Connections, by Shirley Ross, Mary Ann Hawke & Cindy McCord, Morning
    Books,Inc., Palo Alto, CA, 1993
Caps, Hats and Monkeys, by Karen Shackelford, Lasting Lessons, Dallas, TX 1994
Felt Fun, Rita & Myles Jamieson, Newport Beach, CA 1990
Finger Plays & Action Rhymes, by Linda Milliken, Edupress, Dana Point, CA 1996
Fun with the Alphabet, by Jo Ellen Moore & Joy Evans, Evan Moor Corp., Monterey, CA
    1987
How to Make Three-Dimensional Animals, by Jo Ellen Moore & Joy Evans, Evan Moor
    Corp., Monterey, CA 1986
Integrating Beginning Math & Literature, by Carol Rommel, Incentive Publications, Inc.,
    Nashville, TN 1991
Kinder Centers for Reading Readiness, by Claudia Vurnakes, Monday Morning Books,
    Inc., Palo Alto, CA 1995
Learning About Animals, by Jo Ellen Moore & Joy Evans, Evan Moor Corp.,Monterey, CA
    1987
Literature Activities for Young Children, by Dianna Sullivan, Teacher Created Materials,
    Inc., Huntington Beach, CA 1990
Math with Nursery Rhymes, by Kathy Darling, Evan Moor Corp., Monterey, CA 1994
Mother Goose's Animals, by Nancy Polette, Book Lures Inc., O'Fallon, MO 1992
Preschool Teacher's Month-by-Month Activities Program, by Lorraine Clancy, The Center
    for Applied Researvh in Education, West Nyack, NY 1991
600 Manipulatives and Activities for Early Math, by Diane Peragine, Scholastic Inc, New
    York,   NY 1991
Sing and Read Little Books, Color & Theme, by Frog Street Press, Crandall, TX 1997
Spanish Piggyback Songs, by Sonya Karanwinkel, Totline Books, Warren Publishing
    House, Everett, WA 1995
Units Through the Year, by Kitty Ainsworth and Gail Nettles, Carson-Dellosa Publ. Co.,
    Inc., Greensboro, NC 1991

WHY ARE SONGS AND FINGERPLAYS CRUCIAL IN AN EARLY CHILDHOOD CLASSROOM?

Complied by Silvia León

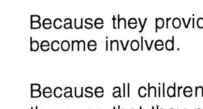

- Because they provide the opportunity for all children to become involved.

- Because all children need to say words in order to acquire them, so that they may be used later on in reading and creative writing.

- Because children become familiar with new words in a meaningful context so that they become part of normal speech.

- Because they motivate children to learn a second language in a stress-free, enjoyable and natural way.

- Because the shy child, who rarely volunteers, can enter into the song or rhyme with all the poise and security of the confident child.

- Because songs and fingerplays are usually conducted in a relaxed, happy atmosphere where learning occurs in the doing (process) and not in the end result (product).

- Because they provide emotional releases and contribute to the general social and emotional stability of children.

- Because songs and fingerplays create a happy bond with other children as well as with their teacher.

WHEN TO USE MUSIC AND RHYMES WITH YOUNG CHILDREN

By Silvia León

- As a motivational activity leading into a lesson (circle time)

- As a follow-up ending of a lesson (circle time)

- As a lesson (circle time activity) in itself

- During transitional periods

- To calm children during a very active day

- To soothe emotions after an emergency (earthquake, riot, illness, etc.)

- Indoors as well as outdoors

- At school or on field trips

- As an independent classroom center

- ANYTIME, ANYWHERE, EVERYDAY!!

CULMINATING PRESENT

By Silvia León

Dear Teachers,

For many years I've given my students cassette presents at the end of the school year and it has been a huge success! This is how I do it:

1. I begin the cassette by recording who I am, what grade level we're in, the name of our school, the school year, what room number we're in and a hello message.

2. Next, I record the voices of my students after they've learned a new song or rhyme. I do this throughout the entire school year and keep the cassette at a listening center where children can independently listen to themselves and their classmates. They love this!

3. When we have recorded all the songs and rhymes, I end the tape with a special good-bye message. (Don't forget to include other good-bye messages from your teacher assistants or teaching partners!)

4. Finally, I buy cassettes at Pic-n-Save and mass-produce one for each of my 30 students.   Ask your administrator if your school owns a cassette duplicating machine. Sometimes equipment like this is hiding in a closet somewhere and nobody uses it. If not, maybe a nearby school will lend you theirs.

5. I photocopy a jacket cover with a title, such as "Songs and Rhymes from my Preschool Days", the name of the school and the year. I add a colorful sticker and each child's name on the cover that I fit inside the outer plastic container of the cassette. And there you have it!

The results are wonderful! Children, as well as their parents, will treasure this cassette as a special "live" memory of their preschool (kindergarten, etc.) days forever!

TEACHER'S NOTES